SKIN HUNGRY

Erin Mallon

BROADWAY PLAY PUBLISHING INC
New York
www.broadwayplaypublishing.com
info@broadwayplaypublishing.com

SKIN HUNGRY
© Copyright 2023 Erin Mallon

Cover art by Qamber Designs & Media

First edition: December 2023
I S B N: 978-0-88145-997-5

Book design: Marie Donovan
Page make-up: Adobe InDesign
Typeface: Palatino

SKIN HUNGRY had its World Premiere at LAB Theater Project (Founder/Executive Director Owen Robertson) in Tampa, Florida, in October 2021. The cast and creative contributors were:

RUTH...Roz Potenza
ROWAN...Darius Autry
JIM ....Eddie Gomez
GINA ....Haley Janeda

Director...Owen Robertson
Stage Manager ....Crystal Reina
Set design ....Owen Robertson
Costume design....................................Beth Tepe-Robertson
Lighting design ....Kristy Pike
Sound design.. Tom Kersey
Scenic Artist ....Beth Tepe-Robertson

NOTE ON MUSIC

For performance of copyrighted songs, arrangements
or recordings referenced in this play, permission
of the copyright owner(s) must be obtained. Other
songs, arrangements or recordings may be substituted
provided permission from the copyright owner(s) of
such songs, arrangements or recordings is obtained,
or songs, arrangements or recordings in the public
domain may be substituted.

CHARACTERS

RUTH, *70s*
ROWAN, *20s*
JIM, *40s*
GINA, *30s*

This play is dedicated to Delphi Harrington, a tremendous actor who has brought such love and life to Ruth over the play's development.

Delphi, you are a playwright's dream.

Scene One

(RUTH *sits alone in a library, surrounded by old-looking books. She "reads" one for a bit, then slowly, slowly lowers her nose to the page.*)

RUTH: *(Sniff sound. Longer sniff sound)* Mmmmm. Oh that's delicious. *(Sniff sound. Longer sniff sound)* Oh God, yes.

ROWAN: Hi.

(RUTH *flings the books off the table.*)

RUTH: *(Startled)* Hi! I'm reading! I'm reading books in the library!

ROWAN: I can...see that. But maybe you should *(He holds his finger up to his lips)* "Shhhh."

RUTH: Yes of course. My apologies.

(ROWAN *gathers the books and places them back on the table.*)

ROWAN: I'm Rowan.

RUTH: Ruth.

ROWAN: You look like a Ruth.

RUTH: Okay.

(Beat)

ROWAN: Do I look like a Rowan?

RUTH: I'm not sure how to answer that.

ROWAN: It means "little red one". What were my parents thinking, right? Little red one? I mean, am I a cardinal or am I a man? I'll go ahead and answer that for you Ruth, I am a man.

RUTH: I can see that, yes.

ROWAN: I gotta ask you though, Ruth: what are you DOING?

RUTH: I was sniffing the books. I was sniffing the hell out of the books.

ROWAN: No, obviously you were. Who doesn't like to sniff books? I meant, like, what are you doing to ME, girl?? I've been following you around on campus this afternoon because you're just so damn radiant.

RUTH: What? That's—

ROWAN: Yeah, I'm drawn to your shit like the earth is drawn to the sun. Wait is that—? Wait. Like the moon is drawn to the earth? Fuck if I know. What I'm saying is that right now, one heavenly bodily is being pulled toward another heavenly body...and somebody's rocket is about to land.

RUTH: *(Rising)* I'm calling security.

ROWAN: That would be me! How can I help?

RUTH: Wait, you're...

ROWAN: Security, yep.

RUTH: Aren't you a little...small for that job?

ROWAN: I'm big where it counts, ladylady.

RUTH: What?

ROWAN: What?

(Beat)

RUTH: *(Gathering her books)* I'm going to go.

ROWAN: Shit. I came on too strong? *(He starts banging his head on the table.)* Stupid! Stupid! Stupid!

RUTH: Oh my! Oh my! Oh my!

ROWAN: Stupid!

RUTH: STOP!

(Beat)

ROWAN: Ruth, I don't mean to be critical, but again, this is the library. Voices down, please.

RUTH: …Rowan?

ROWAN: Yes mam.

RUTH: I feel like you're flirting with me. In a very strange, but undeniably interesting way.

ROWAN: Accurate.

RUTH: Why…?

ROWAN: …am I flirting with you?

RUTH: Yes.

ROWAN: Why wouldn't I?

RUTH: For starters, you're a child and I'm a senior citizen.

ROWAN: Senior citizen, my ass! You're slammin!

RUTH: Thank you. Nevertheless—

ROWAN: You're welcome! Besides. Labels like that mean nothing. My cousin got mail from Aaaaaaaarp! *(Clapping like a seal)* when he turned thirty.

RUTH: Sorry. What?

ROWAN: Aaaaaaaaarp? *(Clapping like a seal).* You know: A-A-R-P. Old people club.

RUTH: Oh. Okay.

ROWAN: Gosh, I'm nervous around you. You a freshman?

RUTH: I mean, it's my first time taking classes here, but I wouldn't call myself—

ROWAN: Killer. I love freshman! I'm a junior. You dig older men?

RUTH: Like…you?

ROWAN: Hell yeah, like me!

RUTH: But you're not actually—

ROWAN: …older than you in *age*, no. But in collegiate wisdom? I got years on you, kid. I could show you a thing or two. *(Quick beat)* Hey, you wanna get out of here? Let's get out of here.

RUTH: I don't think that's—I'm not in a place to— *(Beat)* You know what? Yes.

ROWAN: *(Excited)* Yes??

RUTH: Let's get out of here.

Scene Two

(JIM stands in the doorway of GINA's apartment.)

JIM: Hi.

GINA: Jim?

JIM: Yeah.

GINA: Gina.

JIM: Hi. Thank you for— Should we—I don't know how do you—? Do we shake?

GINA: Sure, we can shake.

(GINA and JIM shake hands.)

JIM: I'm nervous.

GINA: That's okay.

JIM: No like, that is my permanent state. Nerves. My nerves are just...nerving constantly.

GINA: Well that's part of the reason you're here, yeah?

JIM: Yeah. *(Beat)* I think I'll be pretty good at this actually. I went to a rock climbing class once in my twenties and the instructor said my thighs and buttocks are fairly firm. Does that help?

GINA: That has absolutely nothing to do with it.

JIM: Okay. *(Quick beat)* So, should should I...? *(He moves to enter.)*

GINA: BEFORE YOU COME IN!!!

JIM: Yes! Okay! What?

GINA: If you're planning on chopping me up into tiny pieces, you should know that I never see clients without my six-foot-five, two hundred and ninety-seven pound roommate Claude being present in the apartment. He won't bother us, he'll stay in his room the whole time, unless of course he hears my murder beginning, at which point he'll make an appearance, and you'll need to murder him as well, which I can assure you will be a hassle. You don't want a hassle do you?

JIM: No, I—I hate hassles.

GINA: Fantastic. Me too. Come on in then.

JIM: Great. Great. *(He enters. Beat)* So...do we go right to your—oh! Maybe this is not a bed thing? Is this a couch thing? Sorry, I don't know how this works.

GINA: It works however you want it to work. Bed, couch. Your choice.

JIM: Oh. Okay, uh. I think...yeah, you know, let's do the couch thing. I think the couch is...yeah. *(He bounds toward the couch.)*

GINA: I do need to be paid first though.

JIM: Sure! Right! It's…?

GINA: Eighty dollars cash for the hour.

JIM: Of course.

(JIM *hands* GINA *the money.*)

GINA: Thank you. Before we dive in, we need to set the ground rules. And of course, you need to browse the menu.

JIM: Great. Let's take a looky. *(Beat)* Let's do…I dunno, 3? Do you like Number 3?

GINA: It's not about what I like, it's about what you want to experience.

JIM: I think I'd like to experience Number 3. Gosh, 5G looks nice too though. Shit, 8A? You pick you pick you pick, I'm happy with whatever you pick.

GINA: Fair enough. We'll start seated and facing each other. Is that ok with you?

JIM: Sure. Of course.

GINA: Great. *(Beat)* Now let's take a moment, allowing our bodies to settle into the cushions…

JIM: My god you're pretty.

GINA: Oh.

JIM: Is that okay to say? Can I say that to you?

GINA: It's fine. Speaking the truth is encouraged in this space.

JIM: Great. You're pretty.

GINA: Thank you. Okay. First of all, thank you for taking care of yourself.

JIM: You're welcome?

GINA: Are your clothes freshly laundered?

JIM: I'm not sure what—

GINA: When I approach you, will I be welcomed by freshly laundered linen or will I be accosted by soiled slacks and fragrant fabrics?

JIM: Um…

GINA: Either is fine, I just want to be prepared.

JIM: Pretty sure they're…clean-ish cotton? How bout you? There's definitely a smell coming offa you. A good smell, I think. It's…how to describe it? Robust? A powerful, musky sort of—

GINA: Dear god, do not say musky! No woman wants to smell musky!

JIM: I'm saying I like it though! I like your musk!

GINA: IT'S PATCHOULI! IT'S SUPPOSED TO CREATE A RELAXED ATMOSPHERE JIM!

JIM: IT IS GINA! I FEEL SO RELAXED!!!!

(Beat)

GINA: Just. Connect with your breath.

JIM: K.

GINA: May I thread my fingers through yours?

JIM: Sure, yeah.

GINA: Are you ok with my thumb being the uppermost digit in our clasp, or would you prefer it to be yours?

JIM: Sorry, what?

GINA: Well I wouldn't want you to feel dominated by my thumb. My thumb is happy to be second in line if that makes you feel more comfortable.

JIM: Either way is…fine. Can you just—?

GINA: Alright. Here I go.

(Silence. Is JIM enjoying it? Hating it? It's affecting him.)

JIM: You know what, you're right you're right, my thumb would be happiest on top please.

GINA: There you go. See? That's why I asked. Better?

JIM: Yeah, that's better, thank you.

(GINA *and* JIM *sit in silence a few moments.*)

GINA: May I stroke your head?

JIM: Um. This one? Up here?

GINA: Yes, that one. What did you think I—

JIM: No, of course. Stroke my head, this head, yes please.

GINA: I want to be clear here, Jim. I will not be touching you in your bathing suit areas during this session. Or any session. Do you understand that?

JIM: Yes, I—I understand that.

GINA: Good. *(Beat)* I'm stroking your head...your—*this* head.

JIM: Yes.

GINA: How does that feel?

JIM: Nice. It's...tingly and...nice.

GINA: Good. May I place my head on your shoulder?

JIM: Sure, sure.

(GINA *does.*)

GINA: How does that feel?

JIM: Good.

GINA: I notice you're becoming aroused, Jim. What would you like to do about that?

JIM: I'm sorry! I didn't mean to—

GINA: It's okay. It's perfectly natural. We always say "if a client gets an erection or a "her-ection" there's no need to panic.

JIM: Oh good, because I was panicking—

GINA: But we do need to talk about it. This is a safe space Jim, you haven't done anything wrong.

JIM: Great. Though I think you should probably stop stroking me for a minute.

(GINA *stops.*)

GINA: So? What would you like to do about it?

JIM: ...About my...erection?

GINA: Yes.

JIM: Honestly?

GINA: Yes.

JIM: Well...honestly I would like to fuck you with it.

(GINA *leaps to her feet.*)

GINA: Jesus Christ!

JIM: Wrong answer?! Was that the wrong answer???!

GINA: Hell yes that was the wrong answer! You pervert! Get out!

(GINA *starts beating* JIM *with a throw pillow.*)

JIM: I'm sorry! I'm so sorry!

(GINA'*s beating* JIM *toward the door.*)

GINA: Get out!

JIM: I'm not murdering her, Claude! She's yelling but I'm not murdering her!

GINA: Claude doesn't exist you idiot!

JIM: (*Popping his head back in the door*) Oh gosh. He really should, Gina! That's so dangerous you being here by yourself!

GINA: Get! Out!

JIM: You're right. Bye-bye now. Thanks for the— (*Quick beat.*) Bye.

(GINA *slams the door.*)

Scene Three

(*We hear giggling in the dark.* ROWAN *and* RUTH *are outside the library, smoking.*)

ROWAN: Girl, you're so cool. If I could, I'd give you pockets in every skirt you own.

RUTH: You— Why?

ROWAN: The patriarchy is screwing you with lack of pockets, right?

RUTH: Oh. I didn't realize.

ROWAN: Yes! The girls here are always talking about how unfair it is they don't have pockets and we guys do.

RUTH: Well, I uh—

ROWAN: You'll forgive me when I say women brought it on themselves, yeah?

RUTH: How do you—?

ROWAN: Well you get purses, right? You get purses! Now you want pockets too? Sorry, but you outsourced your pockets when you decided to carry purses. True story: I tried carrying a man purse once? The world wasn't ready for it. Worst day of my life. Not true. I've had worse, but truth be told, I've never had a better one than this day here, the day I met you. (*Silence*) No response?

RUTH: Oh. Are you done talking?

ROWAN: Do I talk too much?

RUTH: No actually I—I like it. My husband…isn't much of a talker, so—

ROWAN: Shit, you're married?

RUTH: *Wasn't* much of a talker. Wasn't. Sorry.
Using the past tense just feels…disrespectful to him somehow.

ROWAN: Word. I get that. The spirit lives on and all, right? Like Bruce is probably here with us right now, wondering why I'm hitting on his woman.

RUTH: Sorry…who is Bruce?

ROWAN: Your husband?

RUTH: My husband's name…was Dennis. Why would you think it was Bruce?

ROWAN: I'm intuitive like that. I mean, how cool would that have been if I was right, right? I would've blown your effin mind. I do that at parties and stuff. I don't ask people's names, I just sorta feeeeeeel it out. If a guy looks like a Dave, well then for that moment, he's Dave. I holler out "Dave!! What's up buddy!!?" Most of the time his name ends up not being Dave, but man, when it is??? When his name IS Dave??? That's magic. *(Quick beat)* Doobie?

RUTH: Huh?

ROWAN: Would youbie likey more doobie? I feel like I'm hoggin'.

RUTH: I didn't think young people called them doobies.

ROWAN: I'm not most young people.

(ROWAN *and* RUTH *smoke.*)

ROWAN: So. You diggin HCC?

RUTH: I am.

ROWAN: Classes ya takin?

RUTH: Accounting Principles for Non-Accountants, Figure Drawing 101 and Ethiopian Cuisine for Beginners.

ROWAN: Wow.

RUTH: Well I'm not taking for credit, so...just trying new things. You? What are you taking?

ROWAN: The yooszh. All the requisite stuff.

RUTH: You mentioned being a junior. Isn't community college typically a two-year program?

ROWAN: Yeah. Had to take some time off last year. Got behind. *(Changing the subject)* Got kids?

RUTH: Um. Yes. A son, yes.

ROWAN: Oh man! Lemme guess. He about my age?

(Beat)

RUTH: No. No he's not.

ROWAN: *(Laughing)* Oh good! 'Cause that would be awkward, huh?

RUTH: It would, it sure would!

(ROWAN and RUTH laugh together.)

(It's silent a moment.)

ROWAN: You look sexy when you smoke, Ruth.

RUTH: What are you doing?

ROWAN: What do you mean.

RUTH: With me. Here. What are you doing?

ROWAN: Hangin. Smokin. Flirtin. *(Beat)* I can...stop.

RUTH: No, I—

ROWAN: Haven't you ever felt an immediate connection with someone?

RUTH: ...I have.

ROWAN: Me too. With you. I saw you sniffing the shit out of those books in the library, and for the first time I felt this like…internal pointer finger in my heart just go… (*Aiming and popping his chest in her direction*) "Her. Her. Her! Her! Her!"

RUTH: Ok, wow, that's—

ROWAN: Did you feel it too? With me?

(*Beat.* RUTH *doesn't know what to say.*)

ROWAN: S'okay. From what I understand, I'm an acquired taste.

RUTH: I wouldn't say that. I can taste you right now. I mean. God, I didn't mean— "acquired" just makes it sound like you're not— (*Quick beat*) I only just met you and already I think you're lovely.

(*Beat*)

ROWAN: Damn Ruth, I wanna make out with you. I wanna make out with you all over your face.

RUTH: Oh. …Okay.

ROWAN: Really?! You consent then? Because in today's world it is extremely important that I have your full consent.

RUTH: I—

(ROWAN *grabs* RUTH *roughly by the shoulders.*)

ROWAN: RUTH LOOK DIRECTLY INTO MY EYES AND CONSENT. Ooh. Sorry. That was—I'm excitable I guess.

(ROWAN *strokes* RUTH's *arms gently.*)

RUTH: We're talking about a kiss, right? Just a kiss?

ROWAN: Just a kiss.

RUTH: Then…yes. I— (*Quick beat*) I consent.

ROWAN: Yeah, ya do.

(ROWAN cups RUTH's face. They kiss. It's soft. It's sweet.)

Scene Four

(The next morning. JIM is sitting at his kitchen table eating cornflakes and reading the newspaper.)

RUTH: Morning.

(RUTH kisses JIM's cheek.)

JIM: Morning. *(He kisses her cheek. Beat)* You were out last night.

RUTH: So were you.

(Beat)

JIM: You don't go out.

RUTH: Neither do you.

(Beat)

JIM & RUTH: Where were you?

JIM & RUTH: You go.

JIM & RUTH: No you go.

JIM & RUTH: Well did you have fun?

JJIM & RUTH: I did. Did you?

(Silence)

RUTH: Can I have a hug? You haven't hugged me in… gosh, it's been….

(Beat)

JIM: Sure. Of course. Come here.

(JIM and RUTH hug.)

RUTH: I missed you.

JIM: Missed you too.

RUTH: And not just last night. The past two months have been—

JIM: We haven't been connecting, I know. *(He sniffs.)* Wait. What is…

RUTH: *(She sniffs.)* You smell different…

JIM: So do you. *(He sniffs)* Is that…

RUTH:	JIM:
Patchouli?	Pot?!

(There's a knock at the door. JIM *and* RUTH *break the hug.)*

JIM: Who is that?

RUTH: I don't know.

JIM: We don't get visitors.

RUTH: I know!

(Beat)

JIM: I'll get it. Stay right there. *(He opens the door just a crack.)*

ROWAN: Oh. Hello. I must have the wrong—I'm looking for Ruth?

*(*RUTH *runs to the door and flings it wide open.)*

RUTH: Hi! Hi hi hi.

ROWAN: Oh snap, you're in a bathrobe.

RUTH: *(A bit flirty)* Yeah, well it's early so…

*(*JIM *watches her flirt.)*

JIM: And you are?

ROWAN: Oh hey bro, You can call me Ro. *(Quick beat)* Wan. I'm Rowan. Hahahahaha!

JIM: What kind of a name is Rowan?

ROWAN: It means "little red one."

JIM: Alriiiiiiight.

RUTH: *(To* ROWAN*)* What are you—? Why are you—?

ROWAN: I brought you some books to smell. *(He pats his backpack, which appears loaded.)*

RUTH: Oh wow. That's so…

JIM: Weird. Why is this kid bringing you books to smell?

RUTH: He's just being sweet.

JIM: She doesn't have any money.

RUTH: Yes I do.

JIM: You do?

RUTH: Of course.

JIM & ROWAN: How much?

RUTH: Well—

JIM: Don't answer that! *(To* ROWAN*)* Why do you want to know?

ROWAN: Why do YOU want to know?

JIM: I'm her son.

ROWAN: Oh word? I'm her lover!

JIM: *(Retching sound)* Ew. Oh my god. Ew.

ROWAN: What. "Lover"?

*(*JIM *makes retching sound.)*

ROWAN: *(Patting him on the back)* I'm kidding, man. We haven't slept together!

JIM: Oh thank god.

ROWAN: Yeah no, just some deep kissing and heavy petting at this point, but we'll get there.

(Beat)

JIM: *(To* RUTH*)* What are you—? Dad has only— And this guy is—I mean—he's…he's younger than me.

ROWAN: Considerably.

JIM: Excuse me?

ROWAN: I'm *considerably* younger than you, wouldn't you say? *(To* RUTH*)* You know, you mentioned "the son" to me—

JIM: "The son?"

ROWAN: But the math on this…doesn't really compute.

JIM: What. I'm forty-three. She's—

RUTH: Disclosing! We don't need to be disclosing!

ROWAN: Forty-three? Really?!!

(Beat)

JIM: …Yes?

ROWAN: Bradley Cooper is forty-three.

JIM: Your point?

ROWAN: That… Well, just that…I guess that there are lots of different ways to be forty-three.

(Beat)

JIM: Oh, what a shmuck you are.

ROWAN:	RUTH:
A schmuck! You don't know me.	Don't call him a shmuck!

JIM: Yes, a schmuck!

ROWAN: Listen, I'm not interested in your mom's money, bro. And I'm not looking to be your stepdad, bro. Yet. But I totally appreciate the overprotective thing you're bustin, bro…

JIM: Stop calling me bro.

ROWAN: K. I simply wanted drop these books off for your mom and tell her how special it was meeting her yesterday. *(To* RUTH*)* I don't make new friends easily, so connecting with you meant the world to me. I'm just so thrilled to have a new friend.

RUTH: Me too.

JIM: A friend.

ROWAN: Well I guess if we want to be entirely accurate, she's a FILF. You know, a friend I'd like to—

JIM: Got it. Get out.

RUTH: No. He's staying.

JIM: Momz…

RUTH: This is my house and he's staying.

JIM: Oh, suddenly it's "your" house?

RUTH: It is my house. It always has been.

JIM: Really? Who does the shopping? The cleaning? The bill paying? The laundry? The repairs? Who cooks the meals?

RUTH: You know you seemed so desperate to move out a few months ago, so why are you still here?

(Beat)

ROWAN: I've been wondering the same thing. You know Bradley Cooper doesn't live with his mom, yeah?

JIM: Momz.

RUTH: Why are you suddenly calling me "Momz?"

JIM: Momz, I'm hitting Target on my way home from work today. They're having a sale on Hanes and Maidenform, so I want to get us stocked up. Have you been liking the underwires you've been wearing or do you prefer the Soft Cup Contour?

RUTH: Whichever is on sale is fine.

JIM: Underwires or soft cups.

RUTH: Seriously sweetie, whichever—

JIM: UNDERWIRES OR SOFT CUPS JUST ANSWER ME!

RUTH: SOFT CUPS! SOFT CUPS PLEASE!!!

(Beat)

JIM: Great. Was that so hard?

RUTH: No, it wasn't. Thank you, Jimeny.

ROWAN: Like the cricket?

RUTH: I didn't mean to hurt your feelings. I know you're going through it too and I...well, I love you baby. You know that. You can stay as long as you want to. You know that.

JIM: Love you too. Need anything else?

ROWAN: Yeah... Tampons? Condoms?

JIM: What are you getting at, punk?

ROWAN: Just that there's some...intimacy happening here. You prolly wanna ask her bra size before you go off shopping for her skivvies, yeah?

JIM: She's a 34C, ya punk!

RUTH: Alright now. Jimmy?

JIM: Except in Victoria's Secret! She's a 36C there! They run small! Plus she has a wide ribcage!

(RUTH starts moving JIM toward the door.)

RUTH: Sweetie, thank you! Why don't you head on out now. Thank you!

JIM: You sure you're okay with this guy?

ROWAN: She's more than okay with this guy.

JIM: I'm asking her, ya punk!

RUTH: Enough with the punk stuff! I'm fine. Have a good day, sweetheart.

JIM: But—

RUTH: HAVE A GOOD DAY!

(RUTH *presses* JIM *out and shuts the door.*)

(*Silence as she and* ROWAN *stare at each other.*)

RUTH: Well.

ROWAN: Well. (*Quick beat*) You did say that was your *son*, right? Not your—

RUTH: Yes, my son.

ROWAN: Huh. (*Quick beat*) So you...? (*Quick beat*) Huh. (*Beat*) You got plans this morning?

RUTH: (*Flirty*) Now I do.

ROWAN: Well hold on to your hat, girl. 'Cause things are about to get Lit! erary. (*He dumps the bag of old, sweet-smelling books on the floor.*)

(RUTH *smiles.*)

Scene Five

(GINA *stands in her doorway.*)

JIM: Hi. Thank you for seeing me on such short notice. It's my lunch hour and—

GINA: I have to say, I'm a little surprised we're doing this again.

JIM: Oh yeah?

GINA: ...Yeah.

JIM: Why is that?

GINA: Oh, um. Captain obvious over here, but...it didn't exactly go well the first time.

JIM: It didn't?

GINA: You had an inappropriate sexual response to the platonic touch I was offering you, then you propositioned me, leading me to beat you into the hallway with my Crate and Barrel throw pillows until I could safely slam the door in your face.

JIM: Is that not how sessions usually end?

GINA: I realize this may be a joke to you, but I take my work seriously.

JIM: No, I know you do! And you should!

GINA: This is a calling. A vocation. "I don't do this work for money, I have to take money so I can do this work."

JIM: What does that—? Okay.

GINA: "I am not a heated body pillow."

JIM: Of course you're not.

GINA: These sessions are about helping you "honor your yes and no."

JIM: What does that mean?

GINA: You said you read the website. Did you not read the website?

JIM: No, I did, I did!

GINA: If that were true, you would know these things. (*Quick beat*) You said you had a cuddling emergency, what is your cuddling emergency?

JIM: I, uh—I've had uh—a big change in a... relationship of mine recently and it's throwing me. I'm thrown. I thought everything would be better with this change, but I'm having a hard time letting go and that's been a surprise to me, a really big surprise, because I was so desperate to get out for so long and now that I'm free, actually finally free, I don't know how to deal with it and I find myself wishing I could go back to before, when—

GINA: Shut up for a second.

JIM: Okay.

GINA: Sorry. You were just—you were babbling, and I have a hard time with that. I can only deal with bite size feelings and statements at once.

JIM: ...Okay. Are you sure this is your calling?

GINA: You've had a breakup. Someone broke up with you.

JIM: Not really. Um. She'll...she'll always be a part of my life.

GINA: First love?

JIM: ...kind of? It's complicated.

GINA: I know all about that shit. Do you know I've been out of college for fourteen years? FOURTEEN YEARS and my college boyfriend still weasels his way into my dreams to mess with me at night! Why am I still dreaming about him? He was a douche! It's over! It's been over! My subconscious needs to get the memo and move on!

(Beat. JIM doesn't know what to say.)

GINA: Why are we in the hallway? Get in here. Let's give you some consensual platonic touch to make you feel better.

JIM: Great, thank you. *(He enters her apartment.)*

GINA: Jim, from the moment we're born, the need to be held is established. We're born with it. We cannot thrive without it.

JIM: Oh, are you giving a speech? Should I sit?

GINA: Somewhere along the way, we are told that touch equals sex. Touch does not equal sex.

JIM: I really am sorry about the erection thing.

GINA: Don't interrupt me.

JIM: Sorry.

GINA: A little girl is told not to hug people so much, because they might get the wrong idea about her. A father stops kissing and hugging his son at a certain age and starts giving him handshakes and back slaps instead. So they learn to do without. There is a veritable feast of human beings to connect with on this planet, so why are we all still starving?

JIM: Well, I guess—

GINA: That was rhetorical. Let me speak. A body pressed against another body doesn't have to be sexual. It can be…"a beautiful massage for the soul."

JIM: That sounds wonderful.

GINA: I am open to cuddling clients of all ages of legal consent, all ethnicities, religions, genders and sexual orientations.

JIM: Great.

GINA: What I am not open to are people who disrespect boundaries. Jim? In order to do this work, both you and I must have exquisite boundaries. Yesterday's session was a total shit show. Truth be told, you were my very first client and I didn't know what the fuck I was doing.

JIM: Oh wow, you'd never know it.

GINA: No?

JIM: Yeah no, I felt closer and safer with you than I've felt with anyone in a…a really long time.

GINA: *(Delighted)* Really???!?

JIM: Really.

GINA: That's incredibly sad, but really???!

JIM: Yeah!

GINA: Because that's the whole point of the cuddling movement! To feel closeness. To feel connectedness!

JIM: Well, I felt that with you!

GINA: Great!

JIM: Until you screamed at me, beat me and forced me from your home!

GINA: Right. *(Beat)* Well let's— Let's try again. I'm going to do a better job of creating the space and staying on script.

JIM: Okay.

GINA: Okay. So…I'd like to recommend we begin seated side by side with only our upper arms touching. Do you feel comfortable with that?

JIM: I do.

GINA: "Thank you for being honest with me." Let's settle in.

(GINA and JIM sit side by side and breathe.)

GINA: I'm glad you're here today, Jim.

JIM: Me too.

GINA: "Thank you for taking care of yourself."

JIM: No no, thank YOU.

GINA: I'd like to recommend we lie back and rest our heads on the pillows. Would that be okay with you?

JIM: You know…um.

(Beat)

GINA: Jim?

JIM: Maybe…maybe not yet.

GINA: Oh. Okay. "Thank you for knowing your limits."

JIM: It's not a limit, not like a hard limit, I just feel like…easing in I guess.

GINA: "Thank you for being clear with me." Breathing in… And breathing out… Breathing in… And breathing out.

Scene Six

(RUTH *and* ROWAN *are sitting on the floor, surrounded by books.*)

ROWAN: Oh this one, do this one!

(ROWAN *hands* RUTH *a book. She inhales its pages.*)

RUTH: Dusty, papery must. …Slathered with inky poetry and— *(She inhales again.)* …speckled with side notes of luscious leather.

ROWAN: Damn girl. You make me wanna read. *(Beat. He spots something on her shelf.)* No shit, Scrabble?! You got Scrabble?

RUTH: Of course.

ROWAN: Can we play?

RUTH: …When you grow up, young man.

ROWAN: 'The hell?

RUTH: I just don't think you're ready. To play with me, that is.

ROWAN: Oh really.

RUTH: I have decades of devastation behind me. It won't be any fun for you.

ROWAN: Get out the goddamn board. *(Quick beat)* Sorry! That was so disrespectful. I just really wanna play with you. Can we play, Ruthie? Please???

(Beat)

RUTH: "Ruthie." Um. Alright.

ROWAN: YEAH!!!!

RUTH: But! I warned you.

ROWAN: I've been warned.

RUTH: Why don't you start setting up the game while I get us some snacks.

ROWAN: *(Giddy)* Snacks??? There's gonna be snacks too?

RUTH: Sure.

ROWAN: Score!

(Silence for a bit while ROWAN *sets up the board and* RUTH *gathers snacks and drinks.)*

ROWAN: This is so great! It's so...I dunno...active.

RUTH: Yeah?

ROWAN: Yeah. My last girlfriend and I didn't really do much.

RUTH: Your last— Wait. Am I your—? *(Quick beat)* Forget it. What um, what did you—you and your girlfriend do?

ROWAN: Sat together on the couch and stared at our phones.

RUTH: What about when you went out?

ROWAN: Sat together at a bar and stared at our phones.

RUTH: Ever go to the movies or—?

ROWAN: Sure. Sat together in the dark theater and stared at our—

RUTH: Understood.

ROWAN: Don't get me wrong. I love sitting. And obviously I love staring at my phone, but somehow when I'm with you...? *(He stands.)* I wanna stand. And I want to stare at something far more beautiful than my touch screen. *(He stares her down with intensity.)*

(Beat)

RUTH: Well that's a high compliment.

ROWAN: It is.

RUTH: But sit your ass down, because I'm about to kick it.

(Beat)

(ROWAN *slams his ass into the seat.)*

ROWAN: Let the kicking begin. Choose a tile m'lady…

RUTH: "G."

(ROWAN *picks.)*

ROWAN: "E!"

RUTH: Alright, now you can choose your seven tiles.

(ROWAN *doesn't look at the tiles as he lines them up, his eyes steady on* RUTH *the whole time.)*

ROWAN: Ya know, I think you're underestimating me. Scrabble's in my blood.

RUTH: Oh yeah?

ROWAN: Yeah, I inherited mad vocabularic skills from my grandpa. Grandma always said there's nothing sexier than a man with a big vocabulary.

RUTH: She did?

ROWAN: Well that and a huge cock.

RUTH: *(Sputtering, laughing)* Oh! What? Oh.

ROWAN: *(Laughing)* Did I make you uncomfortable? I'm sorry!

RUTH: No it's fine, it's just—no one has spoken to me like that in…well, ever.

ROWAN: Welcome to me, Ladylady.

(Beat)

RUTH: My turn.

(RUTH *begins picking her letters.* ROWAN *peeks.*)

ROWAN: Aw, I'm sorry. C and V are the real dick letters because you can't make any two-letter words out of them. Good luck with that.

RUTH: Eyes off my tiles young man.

ROWAN: How long do you plan on calling me "young man"?

RUTH: How long do you plan on being twenty-three?

ROWAN: Oh, are you older than me? I barely notice our age difference. Do you?

RUTH: Yes actually, I do, it's—

ROWAN: *(Finally noticing his own tiles)* OH FUCKING COCKSUCKER! SUCK A COCK FULL OF— *(He catches himself. Tries to be adult about this)* Forgive my outburst, Ruth. That was quite…juvenile of me. All but two of my tiles are one pointers, so—

RUTH: That's a good thing! Alien Roast.

ROWAN: 'Scuse me?

RUTH: Alien roast. Those are the letters you always want to have: A—L—I—E—N—R—S—T. You need those in your arsenal so you can have more flexibility on the board. Especially towards the end of the game when it gets harder and harder to connect.

ROWAN: Alright, alright. I got one. First word of the game. P—E—R—P. Perp. *(He lays out his tiles.)*

RUTH: Uh-uh, no. That's an abbreviation.

ROWAN: Is not.

RUTH: Is too.

ROWAN: Nope. Straight up perp!

RUTH: …etrator?

ROWAN: Huh?

RUTH: …etuity?

ROWAN: WHA? I can look it up, want me to look it up? If it's in Urban Dictionary, it counts.

RUTH: No, don't. It's fine. I'll give it to you.

ROWAN: *(Suggestive)* You'll give it to me, will you? Solid.

RUTH: That's not what I—

ROWAN: Hehe. Solid.

Scene Seven

(GINA *is spooning* JIM. *An 80s Hair Band Rock Ballad plays softly.*)

GINA: I love songs about regret. Don't you?

JIM: …No.

GINA: No?

JIM: No. They're sad. They make me feel sad.

GINA: That's what's so beautiful about them.

JIM: That's a pretty privileged stance don't you think?

GINA: You're calling me privileged?

JIM: No no hell no, I wouldn't do that.

GINA: Okay good, because I'll smack a bitch.

JIM: No, I believe you, I do.

(GINA *and* JIM *are still and silent a few moments as they listen to the music.*)

JIM: Was calling me a bitch…"on script?"

GINA: No, it wasn't. I apologize. "Thank you for sharing your truth with me."

(GINA *and* JIM *continue listening to the music and stay connected.*)

JIM: I just meant that someone who loves regretful songs must be lucky enough not have any. And that must be an amazing feeling.

GINA: Well, I wouldn't know.

JIM: Me neither. *(Beat)* You breathe nice.

GINA: "Thank you for noticing my specificities."

JIM: When I was a kid we lived in this little house with steam heat. The radiators were so loud, but I loved it. I thought that sound was the house breathing. I was so comforted by that sound. Made me breathe deeper. Easier.

GINA: That to me sounds like a CO_2 emission. I would have closed my eyes and braced for death.

JIM: I think you mean CO, not CO_2. Carbon Monoxide, yeah?

GINA: Yeah.

JIM: Yeah, Carbon Monoxide is CO, not CO_2. CO, like Colorado. Poor Colorado, huh? And forgive me for man-splaining ever further, but you wouldn't hear a CO emission. Carbon Monoxide is silent. It's the silent killer.

GINA: I like you.

(JIM breaks from the cuddle.)

JIM: YOU DO??! God, I like you too!

GINA: Alright, simmer down now.

JIM: Sorry. Is that okay, am I allowed to like you too?

(Beat)

GINA: Of course you are.

JIM: Oh man, I broke from the cuddle. Should we re-engage the cuddle?

GINA: *(Laughing)* It's fine. We can take a break.

JIM: Will you, um. *(Quick beat)* Will you come to dinner with me tonight?

GINA: Okay, boundaries are all over the place right now, let's just—

JIM: It's just that I have a weekly dinner tonight with the um, well, with the woman I told you about before? And it would mean a lot to have you there with me when I speak to her about some things. It would be … a comfort.

GINA: Oh. Well, we do have the option of an offsite cuddle date…

JIM: Great!

GINA: My usual hourly rate applies.

JIM: Oh.

GINA: Is that okay?

JIM: Yeah, I just thought—

GINA: You thought what.

JIM: No, nothing. That's great.

GINA: Alright, it's a date. "Happy to support you on your journey to vulnerability and self discovery." Oh. Shoot. My phone is buzzing. Do you mind if I —?

JIM: Oh yeah, yeah. Sure.

GINA: I'm sorry, this is so unprofessional, but it could be a new cuddling client and I'm so broke right now it's ridic.

(Beat. JIM looks confused.)

GINA: …ulous?

JIM: Sure, I get the—I guess I just…I never thought about you having other—

GINA: Clients? Of course I have to have other clients. A girl's gotta make a living. *(She picks up and answers*

her phone.) "Be Brave, Be true, Be hygienic too. This is
Gina speaking, how may I touch you?" *(Beat. Her whole
demeanor changes.)* How did you get this number? I
told you not to call me. *Beat.* I don't want to—I have no
interest in—I'm hanging up. No, Dad? I'm hanging—
Don't call me again. Ever, okay? No. I'm done with—
I'm done with— *(Beat)* Goodbye. *(She puts her phone
down.)* Arghhhhhhhhhhuuuuuuuuh! *(Beat)* Okay, sorry
about that. Let's move into an exercise we call "May I,
Will You?"

JIM: Are you okay?

GINA: Fine, thanks. So in "May I, Will You?"—

JIM: That was...your Dad?

GINA: Yes, we don't speak, so—

JIM: Well, it seems like he wants to speak with you.
Why else would he have called?

GINA: I'm not concerned with what he wants, so.

JIM: Why don't you call him back? You only get one
Dad. If I could talk to my Dad, god, in a heartbeat I
would—

GINA: Why don't you stop assuming you know what
you are talking about and telling me what you think
I should do, because I'm pretty sick to death of men
doing that.

(Beat)

JIM: Okay.

GINA: I'm sorry, it's just...these sessions are about you,
not me.

JIM: Right. Of course. How does the...exercise work?

GINA: Great. Let's just dive in. May I...hold your hand.

JIM: ...Yes?

GINA: You tell me, is it a yes?

JIM: Yes.

(GINA *holds* JIM'*s hand.*)

GINA: Your turn.

JIM: May I…kiss you?

GINA: No.

JIM: Too much?

GINA: Yes. Too much. Try again.

JIM: May I…

(Beat)

GINA: You can do a "May I" or a "Will You."

JIM: May I… No. Yeah, this is— *(Quick beat)* Will you…
lay down on your back?

GINA: I will. *(She does.)*

JIM: *(Visibly panicking)* Um…..

GINA: My turn. Will you…tell me what you're feeling
right now?

JIM: Regret.

GINA: Alright. Are you okay?

JIM: I don't…

GINA: Make a request. What would make you feel
more comfortable?

JIM: May I…put on some music?

GINA: Yes you may.

(JIM *connects his ipod to* GINA'*s speakers. A 50s Doo Wop
love song plays.*)

(JIM *turns his back to* GINA *and closes his eyes tightly.*)

GINA: Jim? *(Beat)* Jim?

JIM: Yeah.

GINA: Will you turn around and look at me?

JIM: I will. *(He does.)*

GINA: Go ahead.

JIM: *(On the verge of tears)* May I, um. May I lie down beside you, curl my body around your side and cup your cheek with my hand? I won't do anything else. I promise. I just want to—

GINA: Yes, you may. Of course.

(JIM lies down and snuggles into GINA's side.)

GINA: Okay, let's settle in.

(As soon as GINA and JIM make contact…he sobs uncontrollably.)

JIM: *(Crying)* I'm sorry. I'm so so sorry.

GINA: It's okay, Jim. *(Beat)* May I…touch your hair?

JIM: *(Crying)* Yes please.

(GINA strokes JIM's hair.)

JIM: I'm sorry.

GINA: It's okay Jim. It's okay.

Scene Eight

(The Scrabble board is fuller now.)

ROWAN: M-E-T-A. Meta.

RUTH: …Meta.

ROWAN: Yeah, meta. Like this is so "meta".

RUTH: I don't think that is a word.

ROWAN: Oh it is.

RUTH: It's an abbreviation.

ROWAN: For…?

RUTH: Meta… I don't know. Meta…

ROWAN: I'll look it up.

(ROWAN *whips out his phone.* RUTH *starts rearranging her tiles, frantically, excitedly.*)

RUTH: Wait, wait. I'm not officially challenging you. You only look something up when your opponent is officially challenging you. I'm not willing to lose a turn over this.

ROWAN: No one is losing a turn over— Oh see? Look. Merriam says it's a word.

RUTH: Well in that case... Ooooh! Ha ha ha! Oooooooh. Heeeeeeeee-yah!

ROWAN: What are you—?

RUTH: Wait til you see what I'm going to do, sucka!

ROWAN: *(Reaching to move his tiles)* Oh man, should I not? Am I opening up space for your brilliance?

RUTH: DON'T YOU DARE MOVE THOSE TILES YOU SONOFABITCH!!! *(Quick beat)* Sorry. I love board games.

ROWAN: Never apologize for your passion.

RUTH: Never take credit for my brilliance.

ROWAN: Wouldn't dream of it.

(RUTH *starts laying down her tiles.*)

RUTH: *(Absolutely giddy)* Alright. Now watch me destroy you. I am adding "tarsals" to your "meta"... making "metatarsals", thank you very much, which lands me on a triple word score, giving me *(Counting)* 3, 4, 5, 6, 7, 8, 9, 10, 11, 12, 13 times 3 equals 39... and I've also now connected myself to "quip" to create "quips," another triple word score, thank you very much, giving me *(Counting)* 10, 11, 12, 15, 16 times three equals 48...aaaaaaaaand you may have noticed that I used all seven of my tiles, which is a 50 point bonus, giving me a delicious grand total of…137 points for this most magnificent turn.

(Silence)

ROWAN: You're a force.

RUTH: *(Beaming)* Thank you.

ROWAN: Ever played…dirty scrabble?

RUTH: No. Um. How do you play?

ROWAN: No clue. I'm making it up right this second to celebrate the amazingness that is you. *(He closes his eyes and places his fingers on his temples in concentration.)*

RUTH: Rowan, I don't think—

ROWAN: Here are the rules!! Any time a player spells a body part on the board, the other player gotsta touch it. So…you be getting a foot massage, woman. Slap those tarsals here. *(He holds out his hand.)*

RUTH: You're going to rub my—?

ROWAN: You better believe I am. Put 'em here.

RUTH: Should I take off my socks?

ROWAN: You bet. I want those tootsies in the buff.

RUTH: Okay uh…okay. *(She takes her socks off.)*

ROWAN: There she goes.

RUTH: Just put it…?

ROWAN: In my hand, yeah.

(RUTH places her foot in ROWAN's palm.)

RUTH: *(Startled)* Oh my god!

ROWAN: Did you come? Did I make you come?!

RUTH: No, of course not! That was just…a lot. Can we dial it down a bit?

ROWAN: Sure, yeah. I can do that. *(Quick beat)* You would tell me if I did though, right? If I made you…

RUTH: Sure. Yes. I would tell you.

ROWAN: Cool, yeah. A guy likes to know those things. That better now, what I'm doing?

RUTH: Yes, that's…that's really nice actually.

ROWAN: Good. Good.

(It's silent for a bit as ROWAN *rubs and* RUTH *enjoys.)*

ROWAN: Have you ever thought about how wild it is that you've had the same foot since you were a baby?

RUTH: Uh…

ROWAN: Like this sweet lady foot I have here in my hand is the same exact foot that was kicking around inside your mama. You mom was probably like "Oh hon, she's kicking, she's kicking!" and your dad like waddled over to her—I don't know why I said "waddled," he probably didn't waddle—he *walked* on over to her and put his hand on her belly, hoping and praying to feel this exact foot press into his palm. And then…they both smiled like crazy when it did. This foot got tickled back when it was chubby and stumpy because it had never been stood on before. Then it learned to walk. To jump. It wore shoes. Kicked a ball. Got its toes painted for the first time, wore high heels, took dance lessons… This exact foot has been delighting people for years and years. And now here it is—all these years later—in my hands, delighting the shit out of me.

(Beat)

RUTH: That's incredibly sweet Rowan. And… unexpected.

ROWAN: Like I said, you underestimate me.

RUTH: Maybe I do.

(Silence)

ROWAN: So…do you want to do it?

RUTH: Whaaaat?!

ROWAN: I'm sorry! I'm sorry! Is sex not something you like?

RUTH: Do I not like sex? No, I love sex! I love it so much!

ROWAN: So do I! I feel exactly the same way as you do about this subject!

RUTH: I just—I haven't…experienced it in quite a long time.

ROWAN: How long?

RUTH: …Twenty years?

ROWAN: Twentyyears!?! Shit! Fuck! No, Ruth! No! That's almost as long as my entire life! Let's do it immediately! We have to do it immediately for you!

RUTH: For me?

ROWAN: Yes! I will gladly have sex for you!

RUTH: Um.

(Beat)

ROWAN: Wait, so your husband died twenty years ago?

RUTH: No. Two months ago.

ROWAN: …But you said it's been twenty since—

RUTH: Yeah. We just weren't—he really wasn't— *(Beat)* It's complicated.

ROWAN: Alright. But two months though! Are you okay? Like, should we even be doing this?

RUTH: Yes we should. I should. It's time for me to… *(Quick beat)* Yes.

ROWAN: Okay!

(ROWAN *and* RUTH *crash into one another, Scrabble tiles everywhere.)*

Scene Nine

(GINA *and* JIM *sit in a restaurant at a table set for three.)*

GINA: Do you think maybe she's not coming?

JIM: No, of course she's coming. This is our weekly dine-out.

GINA: Your "dine-out?"

JIM: Yes, our dine-out!

GINA: …Okay. *(Beat)* GINA: Well do you want to text her or something, make sure she's okay?

JIM: She doesn't do the cell phone thing.

GINA: *(Laughing)* "The cell phone thing." Wow. What is she, ninety?

JIM: Seventy-four. Oh! Here she is, here she is. Ohmygod she brought the—

(RUTH *enters with* ROWAN. *Their arms are draped around each other and they look blissfully happy.)*

RUTH: Hi sweetheart! Sorry we're late. Oh! You brought a guest. *(To* GINA*)* Hello.

GINA: Hello.

RUTH: I'm Ruth.

GINA: I'm Gina.

GINA & RUTH: So, you're Jim's…?

ROWAN: *(To* JIM*)* Good to see ya son, is there another chair?

JIM: *(To* RUTH*)* Why is he calling me "son"?

ROWAN: Actually who needs another chair! Come here. Git on my lap, ladylady.

(ROWAN *sits on the third chair and pulls* RUTH *onto his lap, immediately nuzzling her neck.*)

ROWAN: Gina was it? Nice to meet you, I'm Rowan!

(ROWAN *shakes* GINA's *hand.*)

RUTH: (*Giggling as she's being nuzzled*) Yes. Apologies, this is my...this is Rowan.

ROWAN: It means "little red one."

JIM: NO ONE CARES ABOUT THE ETYMOLOGY OF YOUR NAME! (*Beat*) Sorry. Mom, I just didn't realize you'd be bringing—

RUTH: Well, I didn't realize *you*'d be bringing your—

GINA: (*Realizing*) Mom! Have we been talking about your *Mom* this whole—Hold. Up. I hate to ask something so obviously heinous, but did you bring me here to make your *Mom* jealous?

JIM: Yes. No. No! I just wanted her to see that I have a— That I can function outside of—

GINA: That's it. You CLEARLY have not read the code of conduct on the website. It's not your fault. It's my responsibility to have exquisite boundaries and CLEARLY I don't. CLEARLY I'm terrible at my job. I'm calling an Uber. (*She pulls out her phone.*)

JIM: Gina, I need you. Please stay? Mom? I got your favorite Pinot. Drink up.

(JIM *pours a glass for* RUTH *and she immediately starts sipping with gusto.*)

RUTH: Thank you sweetheart.

ROWAN: Rrrrrrrrrrrrrrrr. Shit.

RUTH: What?

ROWAN: I haven't checked my phone in hours because I've been so hyped up and satiated by your lady loving...

(JIM *makes a retching sound.*)

ROWAN: ...but now that she's looking at her phone? I'm feeling like... Rrrrrrrrrrrrrrrrr.

RUTH: Look at your phone sweetheart. I don't mind.

ROWAN: Really? Because I don't want you to doubt my affection and attention for a second. You're the only eye candy I need.

RUTH: Awww. That's so sweet.

ROWAN: You're so sweet.

RUTH: You're so sweet.

ROWAN: You're so sweet.

RUTH: You're so sweet

ROWAN: You're so sweet.

RUTH: You're so sweet.

ROWAN: You're so sweet.

RUTH: You're so—

JIM: CHECK THE PHONE, LITTLE RED!!!!

ROWAN: Thanks for the term of endearment, Jimeny, that means a lot.

JIM: I wasn't—

ROWAN: Arrrrrgggghguddahguddah! (*He has let out a primal sound as he unleashes his phone.*)

GINA: Yeah, I'm sticking around, this is way too interesting.

(ROWAN *starts scrolling through his phone like a beast.*)

ROWAN: (*Under his breath*) 15 likes...7 retweets... Ooh! Sweet hashtag! (*Typing*) "Holla back, bro, catch ya on the flip yo." "Ho ho, yer insta game is strong, fellafella!"

RUTH: *(To* JIM*)* Sweetheart, I brought Rowan with me tonight, in hopes that you two can get to know each other better. I think when you do, you'll find that you actually have quite a lot in common.

(ROWAN *puts his phone down and his hands up.)*

ROWAN: Whew! Alright, dunzo. Fuck, for a second there I felt like my organs were being squeezed dry, ya know? I needed the juice of technology to hydrate my insides and water my FOMO away.

JIM: I have absolutely nothing in common with this man.

GINA: That can't possibly be true.

RUTH: If you haven't realized it yet, my son is quite contrary. If you say something is up, he'll immediately say it's down. He's always been that way. Even when I was pregnant with him he would—

GINA: You've both been inside Ruth!

JIM: Whaat???!

GINA: That's what you and Rowan have in common.

RUTH: Wow. Wow, that's—

ROWAN: Yikes, that's some risky humor, lady.

GINA: In different ways of course. *(To* JIM*)* You were gestating and *(To* ROWAN*)* you were—

JIM: WE GOT IT. GINA, WE GOT IT.

(Silence)

(They all sip wine.)

ROWAN: Speaking of gestating… Can I do that thing no one ever wants you to do where I show you picture of a baby I love deeply who you don't particularly care about but need to show intense interest in or else you run the risk of appearing like an unfeeling asshole?

RUTH, GINA & JIM: Sure…

ROWAN: Great! This is Raina, my niece. She's a month old. (*He holds his phone out to them.*)

RUTH, GINA & JIM: Aw. She's beautiful.

ROWAN: Thanks, I know, right? I went to meet her the week after she was born. I brought my brother and his wife a Tupperware container filled with beefaroni. I love beefaroni and apparently putting food in a Tupperware container really hits it home to the new parents that you care. I googled "how to support new parents" and learned that little tidbit. Oh and for the record, you're not supposed to ask for the Tupperware back. Just let em keep it, so make sure it's not something youre too attached to. Anyway, I get there and they get me all propped up with pillows on their fancy couch, then they plop little Raina in my arms. And know what she did? Her little hand instantly wrapped around my finger. Tight. Here, Ruthie, give my finger a little squeeze.

(RUTH *wraps her hand around* ROWAN's *index finger.*)

ROWAN: Yeah, just like that! Like she trusted me. Like she knew I was good people. Knew she was safe with me. I was so moved and grateful, I almost cried all over her little baby body. Meant a lot to me, ya know? Like she's the only person besides my mom, and now Ruth, who doesn't always assume I'm a fuck up. And since my mom passed I've been feeling a little—

(RUTH *lets go of* ROWAN's *hand.*)

RUTH: Wait. Your um. Your mom passed?

ROWAN: Yeah. Oh, did I not mention that?

RUTH: No. You didn't.

JIM: When?

ROWAN: Huh?

JIM: When did your mom pass? And, my condolences.

ROWAN: Thanks. Over the summer.

RUTH: That's…recent.

ROWAN: I guess.

(Silence)

(JIM and GINA look at RUTH.)

RUTH: You know what, I could use my own chair.

JIM: Here Mom, take mine.

(RUTH gets off ROWAN's lap and takes her own seat. JIM stands.)

JIM: The timing of this relationship suddenly seems a little—

GINA: Leave them alone, Jim.

JIM: 'Scuse me?

GINA: They're happy. They're having fun.

ROWAN: That's right, we're having fun, aren't we Ruthie?

RUTH: We are, yes. *(She chugs her wine and pours more.)*

JIM: Mom, you don't find it strange that as soon as he loses his mother, he—

GINA: Can I say what we're all thinking? You seem a little…attached…to your mom, Jim. A little…jealous? A little…

JIM: No, I'm not jealous, I'm concerned, I'm—

ROWAN: Agreed! He seems a little sad too, wouldn't you say? He drags himself around like life is such a slog.

JIM: Well life ain't no rainbow jump rope, Rowan.

ROWAN: No, but I mean, literally. You literally...drag a bit when you walk.

GINA: I've noticed that! Like in sad little circles?

ROWAN: Yes!

JIM: *(Under his breath)* Geeeeee-zuz. make it stop.

ROWAN: Like his feet are little boats with broken rudders so they end up just kinda slappin around... *(He demonstrates by slapping his foot on the floor.)*

RUTH: Oh, there's a
reason for that. He has   JIM: I have inserts in my
inserts in his sneakers.   sneakers.

GINA: Those actually aren't great for you.

JIM: What aren't? My inserts?

GINA: Yeah. You're shoving something in your shoes to lift you up, when your instep should be strong enough to lift itself. Can I see it? Your instep? We can work on the emotional life of your instep in our next session.

JIM: Excuse me, I need a minute to... Um. I just need a minute. *(He walks away from the table. He definitely drags a bit like his feet are sad little, broken-ruddered boats.)*

RUTH: Jimeny!

ROWAN: *(Patting RUTH's hand)* Hon. I got this.

Scene Ten

(JIM stands at a urinal.)

JIM: "Little boats with broken rudders." I'd like to see your rudder broken, you piece of— "You seem a little attached Jim, a little—" What the hell do these people know about—

(The door opens. ROWAN saunters into the bathroom and takes the urinal directly beside JIM.)

ROWAN: Hey man.

JIM: Are you kidding me right now.

ROWAN: What.

JIM: Every man knows it's bad form to take the middle when the one on the right is available. What are you doing?

ROWAN: Urinating. At a urinal.

JIM: Yeah but you gotta give people space—

ROWAN: Do people need space? Or do they need closeness? Wah-pooh! *(He completely drops trou, his pants hitting the floor.)*

JIM: Unnecessary! It is one hundred percent unnecessary to completely drop trou!

ROWAN: *(Very reasonable)* You just said people need space. Alright then, I need vertical space to excrete. I'm not ashamed of my member like you apparently are, tucking it between your sad flaps of denim, barely releasing your stream…

JIM: Whaaat?! Shut up!

ROWAN: Is standing next to me making you feel inadequate?

JIM: No! Why? Are you—?

ROWAN:	JIM:
Ohmygod you peeked!	Ohmygod I peeked!

ROWAN: You're never supposed to peek!

JIM: You don't think I know that?! You were goading me!

ROWAN: I did not "goad".

JIM: You did! You wanted me to look!

ROWAN: Well?

(Beat)

JIM: Well what?

ROWAN: *(Dropping his voice low)* Do you like what you see? *(Beat. Laughing)* I'm kidding, dude! Oh man!

(ROWAN slaps JIM on the back, nudges his shoulder.)

JIM: Touching me, there's so much touching me.

ROWAN: *(Backing off)* Ah. Sorry, Always been a touchy feely guy, I guess. You're right. Zip up brother, zip up.

JIM: Let's not with the "brother" thing.

ROWAN: Alright. Son?

JIM: How about Jim.

ROWAN: K. You a hand washer?

(JIM and ROWAN zip and move toward the sinks.)

JIM: Um. YES.

ROWAN: Great. Hashtag Me too. Wait, no. That's something different. I don't... *(Quick beat)* Ya know, I'm realizing that I don't always say the right thing.

JIM: Oh no?

ROWAN: No. And ya know, I think it gets in my way? People have a real easy time dismissing me as just some dippy kid.

(JIM and ROWAN wash their hands.)

JIM: I wonder why that is.

ROWAN: Because I say such stupid shit, man! But here's the thing: I don't even know it's perceived negatively until it's out in the open, like...wafting around and offending everyone. *(Quick beat)* It's like...do you ever catch a whiff of your armpit and it shocks you? Like *(He sniffs under his arm.)* you just can't believe that that smell is coming from you because you thought you were relatively clean? It's like that.

JIM: *(Referencing his armpit)* You smell right now?

ROWAN: No. I was doing a re-enactment for you.

JIM: Oh, thank you.

ROWAN: Sure thing, Jim. You know, that's one of the reasons I like your mom so much. She lets me be me. *(Quick beat)* I think I love her man.

JIM: Oh, gimme a—

ROWAN: And I know what you were all insinuating back there, thinking that losing my mom is what draws me to Ruth. But that's some bullshit. Situations couldn't be more different. I miss my mom and like being her son, but *your* mom? Your mom makes me want to run through a big field, tear my shirt open then roll around in the dirt until it gets stuck in all the cracks and creases of my body so anybody who takes one look at me would be like "Wow, you've had a day, huh?" She makes me wanna jump into a big ass body of water, squish the sandy bottom with my big toes, then gather a shit ton of seashells and make necklaces for all my friends. She makes me wanna jump out of a car while it's still moving and-

JIM: Are you drunk?

ROWAN: Not at all. *(Beat)* But do ya wanna be? *(He opens his jacket to reveal many tiny bottles of booze.)*

Scene Eleven

(RUTH and GINA wash their hands in the ladies' restroom.)

RUTH: So. Ginny.

GINA: Gina.

RUTH: Ginny, is my son a powerful lover?

(GINA chokes on her own spit sound.)

RUTH: I'm certain he is. His father was. A cold lover. But powerful. That sort of thing is hereditary, isn't it?

GINA: I have no idea.

RUTH: I'm certain it is.

GINA: No, I mean, I have no idea if—

RUTH: We opted not to circumcise him you know. Of course you know, you've— Anyway, it was a bold move for the Seventies because everyone was lopping it off back then. People thought we were nuts. Negligent. "Aren't you worried about keeping it clean?" and "But doesn't Dennis care that they will look different?" I always thought…why? Are there going to be father and son penis portraits in our future? In what world does it matter if a father and son have identical penises?

(Beat)

GINA: Ruth. I think there's been a mistake. I'm not your son's girlfriend. I am his cuddle therapist.

(Beat)

RUTH: Hahahaha!

GINA: I'm serious.

RUTH: Oh. Is that a thing? I didn't realize that was a thing.

GINA: It is. It's a thing.

RUTH: So…is it like being a prostitute but with cuddling instead of coitus?

(Beat)

GINA: No Ruth, it's more like being a massage therapist but instead of deep tissue work, I offer healing, consensual, non-sexual touch.

RUTH: Oh. That sounds very nice actually.

GINA: It can be.

RUTH: And that's what you're doing with my son?

GINA: Yes.

RUTH: At dinner?

GINA: Well, we also offer offsite cuddle dates where— *(Quick beat)* Are we done here?

RUTH: Sure, sure.

GINA: Great. I'll um—I'll see you back at the table.

(GINA goes to leave, but RUTH stops her.)

RUTH: Why does he—why doesn't he— Don't I offer him—

GINA: Ruth, I'm not at liberty to discuss Jim's case with you.

RUTH: His case? Why does he have a— Oh my lord you have gorgeous skin.

GINA: Oh. Um. Thank you.

RUTH: May I touch your skin?

GINA: I don't think— Oh, there you go, you're touching it.

(RUTH is cupping GINA's cheek. GINA freezes, but lets her.)

GINA: I guess I'm glad I witnessed you washing your hands.

RUTH: *(Stroking her cheek)* You're so young.

GINA: Not that young actually.

RUTH: No, you're young.

GINA: So why is everyone trying to sell me Rodan and Fields "Reverse" anti-aging cream?

RUTH: Are they?

GINA: Ruth, every woman in her early to mid-thirties is trying to sell me Rodan and Fields "Reverse" anti-aging cream. It's depressing. Not just the fact that we're on a constant quest to smooth out our faces, but why does every woman my age sell this shit and want me to sell it too?

RUTH: Does it work?

GINA: It's fucking fantastic. My fine lines and crow's feet have all but disappeared after six months of using the product.

RUTH: *(Really examining her)* Yeah, I don't see any.

GINA: Thanks, it's exciting!

RUTH: No smile lines either.

GINA: 'Preciate that. Yeah, I curbed the smiling a few years ago when I saw the havoc it was wreaking around my lips. *(Beat)* How do you deal with it? Getting older?

RUTH: Well, we're all doing it, aren't we?

GINA: Yeah but I mean you…you're really doing it. I mean! You've just been doing it longer. I mean! *(Quick beat)* Are you interested in joining our community of entrepreneurs and experiencing healthier, younger-looking skin and connections with great people? At Rodan and Fields, success comes from creating meaningful connections-

RUTH: Oh. Are you also selling Rodan and Fields?

GINA: I am selling the shit out of it, Ruth. If things keep moving in this direction I'll be able to stop cuddling soon. Are you interested in learning more about "the opportunity?"

RUTH: No thank you sweetheart.

GINA: K.

(RUTH is looking GINA up and down. It's silent a moment.)

GINA: Um. Are you okay? The way you're looking at me is a little…

RUTH: Fine yeah, just maybe had a little too much wine at dinner. Gosh, you have such a sweet little figure. I used to have a figure like that.

GINA: I'm not gonna lie. Things are pretty tight.

RUTH: I can tell. I can tell they're tight. That's wonderful for you, congratulations.

GINA: Thank you.

Beat. RUTH *looks a bit dreamy, misty-eyed.)*

GINA: You're not going to—I mean, we're not going to kiss, are we?

RUTH: I don't think so. I'm just…

(Beat)

(GINA tries to gently move away from RUTH and toward the door.)

GINA: Should we…? How about we…go?

RUTH: Yes. You're right. Let's—let's go see what our boys are doing.

Scene Twelve

(Inside the community college library. After hours. It's dark.)

JIM: What the hell are we doing—?

RUTH: Shhh…we're being wild, baby.

JIM: Oh, okay. We're being wild.

GINA: *(To ROWAN)* How do you have the keys to this place?

RUTH: *(Proud)* Security. He's security. *(To GINA)* Sexy, huh? He's the guy with the keys.

ROWAN: Side gig. Has some perks.

GINA: Aren't there cameras? Won't you get caught?

ROWAN: Switched 'em off. We're all good.

GINA: But don't you feel guilty breaking in? For using your—

RUTH: Sweetheart, men don't feel guilt.

JIM: What?

RUTH: They don't.

JIM: Are you kidding me right now? I feel guilt constantly. But that's the way you like me, isn't it? That's the way your life works best?

RUTH: Sweetie, did you drink too much? What in the world are you talking about?

ROWAN: And…let there be light!

(The lights in the library go on.)

ROWAN: Nips for everyone!

(ROWAN passes around miniature bottles of booze.)

JIM: Nips?

ROWAN: Yeah, mini booze bottles are called nips.

GINA: I didn't know that. Nips?

ROWAN: Nips.

RUTH: Nips?

ROWAN: Nips.

RUTH: Everybody raise their nips!

GINA & ROWAN: Raise your nips!

JIM: STOP SAYING NIPS!!!!

(Beat)

RUTH: Sweetheart, we're celebrating.

JIM: What, Mom. What are we celebrating.

ROWAN: Life! New friends! Love! Take your pick, pal.

JIM: Rowan? I need you to stop. I'm not your bro. I'm not your son. I'm not your pal. I am simply the son of the elderly woman you happen to be fucking.

RUTH: Elderly!

GINA: Whoa, Jim, whoa!

ROWAN: Have some respect for your mother, Jim.

(Beat)

JIM: Respect? Two months after she loses her husband—two months! —You sweep in like some freaky little John Stamos to romance her and what. What the hell are your intentions with her?

ROWAN: John Stamos? Who the hell is John Stamos?

JIM: You said the security thing is a side gig.

ROWAN: …Yeah?

JIM: On the side of what?

ROWAN: Oh um. Well, I guess it's the *only* gig right now, but—

JIM: Gotcha.

RUTH: *(To JIM)* He's in school, sweetheart, go easy.

JIM: I just feel like if he's going to be providing for you now, he should have some solid employment in place. Because I'm done being the family cash cow.

RUTH: Cash cow— And he's not "providing" for me. We're just—

JIM: Do you know she is seventy-four years old?

ROWAN: I figured she was around that age—

JIM: Seventy-four years old and running around with a punk kid who breaks into the community college library to get wasted. It's ridiculous. It's embarrassing.

(*To* RUTH) What do you think dad would think about this?

RUTH: I don't give a shit what your dad would think!!!! (*Silence*) Your father turned his back to me for years.

JIM: What do you—

RUTH: Every night. His back turned to me. He was cold. He was like talking to and touching a wall. Never heard me. Never listened. "Did you hear what I said, Dennis? Dennis, did you hear me?" Everything I ever said to him had that follow-up question. In that way, life wasn't much different after the accident happened. I was still speaking to someone who I wasn't sure was listening, but at least then, there was a reason for his silence that I could understand. God, I think I felt—ya know, I think I felt closer to him in that state, because at least I could hope, pretend that we were the couple I wanted us to be.

(*Beat*)

JIM: Oh, did you not pick up on that? Yeah, Mom let a man wither away unconscious in bed for twenty years.

RUTH: I did not let him "wither"! I took care of him. I devoted my life to him.

JIM: And I devoted mine to you. Twenty-three years old and my life stopped completely.

RUTH: That was your choice. You chose to stay and help and—

JIM: Really, Mom? Did I choose to become your de facto life partner? Every doctor, every specialist we spoke to recommended we let him go. But you were selfish. You hung on. And you hung on me to make your life work.

RUTH: You didn't see him! You didn't see him the day that tear slid down his cheek.

JIM: ..."the day that tear slid down his cheek." Yes mom. I know. You never stop talking about that day. But it was fifteen years ago. Happened once. It was never going to happen again.

RUTH: *(To* ROWAN *and* GINA*)* One night I had this idea to play him his favorite song, thinking maybe it would stir something in him. And it did! He could hear it. He could feel it. A tear slid down his cheek. He was alive in there. He was just stuck. I was waiting for him to...

(Beat)

GINA: Gosh this is—I feel like this is way too personal. I think we should— *(To* ROWAN*)* We should go. Want to go?

ROWAN: Nah, I'm not leaving her.

JIM: How long was I supposed to press pause on my life? How many nights was I supposed to sit trapped on the couch with you and Judge Judy, praying for the man upstairs to open his eyes? How long was I supposed to play house with you? Do you know I haven't been with a woman in twenty years? I don't know how.

ROWAN: ...Fuuuuuuuuck, dude.

JIM: Yeah, I pay this woman to let me touch her!

GINA: *(To* ROWAN*)* It's not like that. It's platonic, consensual touch.

ROWAN: That sounds really nice actually.

GINA: It can be. Would you like my card?

ROWAN: Yes actually—

JIM: DO NOT GIVE HIM YOUR CARD HE CAN'T HAVE EVERYTHING!

(Beat)

RUTH: Sweetheart? I'm sorry that this has been such a hard time for you. I'm sorry that it hurts you to see me happy—

JIM: It's not that, Mom, I want you to be—

RUTH: But you know what I think? You were comfortable when you were "trapped" with me. As long as you were "trapped" with me you could pretend I was the one in your way. As long as you were "trapped" you didn't have to try. To be in the world. To be with people. And now you are. You're trying and you're realizing it's not always so easy. Rowan's impulse is joy. That's where he goes first. I can honestly say I've never met someone like that. I know I've never been like that. And… I want that in my life. *(To* ROWAN*)* I want you in my life.

ROWAN: Music to my ears, ladylady.

(Silence)

GINA: I think I can help here.

JIM: I don't have any more cash on me.

GINA: Jim? It's okay. It'll be pro bono.

ROWAN: Heh. "Bono."

RUTH: *(To* ROWAN*)* Sweetie? *(She shakes her head as if to say "not now".)*

GINA: Jim.

(Beat. JIM *is staring off into space.)*

GINA: Jim?

JIM: Yeah. Jim.

GINA: Will you take a comfortable seat on the floor?

JIM: Um. Yeah. I will. *(He does.)*

GINA: Ruth?

RUTH: Yes.

GINA: Will you take a comfortable seat directly in front of your son?

(*Beat*)

RUTH: I will. (*She sits cross-legged in front of* JIM.)

GINA: Rowan? Will you sit directly in front of Ruth?

ROWAN: I will indeed.

(ROWAN *sits in front of* RUTH. *They're now in a mini-massage train of sorts.*)

GINA: Jim will you place your hands lightly on Ruth's shoulders and Ruth will you place yours gently on Rowan's?

JIM & RUTH: I will.

(*They do.*)

GINA: Beautiful. Now let's just sink into this moment. Allow your skin to soak up the sensation. We don't need words here, we don't need anything but our breath and our—

ROWAN: Hold up. I'm not touching Jim.

JIM: That's fine.

ROWAN: No man it's not fine. Gina, I feel like for this dope exercise to work I need to be touching Jim.

GINA: Alright Rowan, how would you like to touch Jim.

RUTH: Rowan, sweetheart, I think maybe we should—

JIM: No it's fine. I got it, I got it. (*To* ROWAN) Gimme your finger.

ROWAN: What's that, bro?

JIM: Send your finger back this way.

GINA: "Will you send your finger…"

JIM: "Will you send your finger back this way."

ROWAN: My finger?

JIM: Yeah, your finger.

ROWAN: What do you plan on doing with my—

JIM: Just do it!

GINA: *(Soothing)* Easy….

(ROWAN sends his index finger past RUTH and towards JIM.)

(It's silent and still a moment as JIM stares at it.)

ROWAN: Alright. Now what are you gonna do? Pull it? Smell it?

JIM: You said before that when your niece… Well, she made you feel like…

ROWAN: Oh.

JIM: So, um. If you want, I mean, I'd be happy to, um. *(Quick beat)* "May I hold your finger."

(Beat)

ROWAN: You may.

(JIM wraps his hand around ROWAN's finger. The three of them stay physically connected and breathing, eyes closed. GINA watches and smiles.)

Scene Thirteen

(Two months ago. JIM and RUTH are on the couch, wrapped up in a blanket watching television.)

RUTH: I just love her. Judy? I just love you! Don't you just love her?

JIM: I dunno mom, she's a bit…much. Don't you think?

RUTH: You wouldn't say that if she were a man. Only women are ever referred to as "too much." If Judge Judy were a man, he'd be just the right amount of

much. Oh, I just love her. Don't you just love her?
As long as she's on the air you know justice is being
served. At least on CBS. You know that people who
don't like her don't like her because she's definitive,
right? Definitive is dangerous in a woman. A woman is
supposed to waver. Makes everyone more comfortable
around her. But a man? A man must be definitive or
we think he's… soft. Sweetheart, can you brush my
hair?

(Beat)

JIM: Sure. Yeah.

(RUTH hands JIM her brush. He takes it as she positions her head in his lap. He starts brushing her hair.)

RUTH: Make sure you get this side too.

(JIM brushes.)

RUTH: And this side too.

(JIM brushes.)

RUTH: And don't forget the back.

(JIM stops brushing.)

JIM: Mom, I'm— *(Quick beat)* I can't—

RUTH: You okay Jiminy?

JIM: Yeah. I'm gonna—I'm just gonna head upstairs.
Lie down for a few.

RUTH: Oh yeah? *(She sits up.)*

JIM: Yeah. Don't worry, I'll be back for the ruling.

RUTH: You sure? Because I can pause for you.

(Beat)

JIM: I know you can. *(He exits.)*

(Lights shift.)

(JIM *enters a room where a man lies in bed attached to machines. He appears to be in a deep sleep.*)

JIM: Hey big guy. I know I haven't been up to see you in a while. It's um. It's just gotten hard for me…to see you like this. To see her like— To see me like— (*Quick beat.*) Well, it's been…hard. (*He watches him for a while.*) You okay? Maybe want to hear some of your music, pal?

(*No response*)

(JIM *moves to the stereo and presses play on an old cassette.*)

(*The same 50s Doo Wop song comes on from earlier.*)

(JIM *turns his back to the man and closes his eyes tightly.*)

JIM: Can you hear that Dad?

(JIM *turns and watches him very closely for any sign of… anything while the music continues to play.*)

(*Nothing*)

JIM: Can you hear it?

(*Nothing*)

JIM: (*Breaking*) Are you in there?

(*Nothing*)

JIM: Okay.

(JIM *takes deep breaths as he makes his decision.*)

(*He goes to the plug in the wall, coming from the machine.*)

(*He wraps his hand around the plug…and pulls.*)

(*He climbs into the bed with the man.*)

(*He lies down beside him, curls his body around his side and cups his cheek with his hand.*)

JIM: Okay. (*He closes his eyes and waits.*)

END OF PLAY

www.ingramcontent.com/pod-product-compliance
Lightning Source LLC
Chambersburg PA
CBHW070027110426
42741CB00034B/2653